IMPRISONED
WITHIN

Stuck in *Un*forgiveness

KIMBERLY NIXON

Copyright © 2016 by Kimberly Nixon

Imprisoned Within
Stuck in Unforgiveness
by Kimberly Nixon

Printed in the United States of America.

ISBN 9781498474597

All rights reserved solely by the author. The author guarantees all contents are original and do not infringe upon the legal rights of any other person or work. No part of this book may be reproduced in any form without the permission of the author. The views expressed in this book are not necessarily those of the publisher.

Unless otherwise indicated, Scripture quotations taken from the King James Version (KJV) – *public domain*.

Scripture quotations taken from the Holy Bible, New Living Translation (NLT). Copyright ©1996, 2004, 2007 by Tyndale House Foundation. Used by permission of Tyndale House Publishers, Inc.

Scripture quotations taken from the Amplified Bible (AMP). Copyright © 1954, 1958, 1962, 1964, 1965, 1987 by The Lockman Foundation. Used by permission. All rights reserved.

www.xulonpress.com

Dedication

I dedicate this book in loving memory of my mother, Elder Juanita Jenkins, who went to be with the Lord on August 7, 2015. My mother was a strong woman with resilience and great passion for service and ministry. Words alone cannot express the impact my mother had on the lives of our family. There will always remain a place in our hearts for her memory and the immeasurable legacy she leaves behind. My mother was known for her powerful anointed voice that blessed all who heard her sing. I believe that her voice continues to resound in the corridors of heaven and one day I'll hear her again. My mom truly found peace in the valley.

In the words of my mother's favorite Negro spiritual;

If when you give the best of your service
telling the world that the Saviour has come
be not dismayed when men don't believe you
He'll understand and say well done.
Oh when I come to the end of my journey,
weary of life and the battle is won.
Carrying the staff and the cross of redemption
He'll understand and say well done.
Lucie E. Campbell

Homegoing Celebration for Elder Juanita Jenkins
"Down to The Last Drop"
Eulogist: Apostle William T. Ford
Williams Chapel Church
Spring Lake, N.C.
August 14, 2015

For I am now ready to be offered, and the time of my departure is at hand. I have fought a good fight, I have finished my course, I have kept the faith: Henceforth there is laid up for me a crown of righteousness, which the Lord, the righteous judge, shall give me at that day: and not to me only, but unto all them also that love his appearing. (2 Timothy 4:6-8)

Elder Juanita Jenkins lived a life poured out in service to God. To be absent in the body is to be present with the Lord. Death is not the end. She has exited this world to enter into the next. She has left one state to enter into the next state. The sting of death is gone because of the victory we have received through Jesus Christ. What a blessing that Elder Jenkins was ready to be poured out. She didn't leave here full, she was empty. She had done all that she was supposed to do in this life. A true servant of the Lord does not leave here until their work is done. We are each given a purpose and a season in which to accomplish that purpose. Once we have fulfilled that purpose, there is no reason to remain here. We are to make sure we align our days with our assignments. We are to be purpose driven and leave here empty having been poured out in His service. Elder Jenkins finished the work and fulfilled her purpose.

Her life was a life worth remembering. She left a legacy to those of us who are left behind. She has made her departure. Departure is a naval term which means to set sail. We say good bye on this side and hello on the other side. She has folded up her earthly tent and moved on to another place. Departure is also an agricultural term which means to take the yoke off of the back of working animals. Elder Jenkins has set sail, folded up her earthly tent, and has laid down all of her heavy burdens. Now she can enter into her well-deserved rest.

A young child asked her mother if it hurts to die. The young mother prayed and asked the Lord how to explain death to her young daughter. What the Lord gave her is a comfort to us all.

"Honey, do you remember falling asleep on the couch watching TV with your father and I and waking up the next morning in your room? Well, your father gently picked you up and carried you as you slept into your room. Death is like that. Jesus comes and carries you to heaven to your new room."

Jesus told His disciples, "I go to prepare a place for you." Elder Jenkins has been carried in the arms of Jesus to her new room.

She lived a committed faithful life that was poured out little by little unto the Lord until there was not a drop left. Her departure from here was not the end. She has been resurrected to a brand new life. She fought the good fight, she finished her race, and has now received the crown of righteousness that had been laid up for her. We know the Lord Jesus carried her to where she was welcomed into God's presence.

Table of Contents

Acknowledgments xi
Introduction: Forgiveness and the Family xiii

Chapter 1: Uprooting the Root of Bitterness 23
Chapter 2: Seemingly Stuck....................................... 37
Chapter 3: Unforgiveness Blinds Vision 49
Chapter 4: Padded Pain 61
Chapter 5: Basis for Forgiveness................................. 75

Conclusion: Unfinished Business Underneath Unforgiveness 87
About the Author... 93

Acknowledgments

As I continue on my journey of discovering the life changing power of God's grace, I am grateful for the wonderful family and friends that continue to enhance and bless my life.

My process of growth would not be where it is today if it had not been for my loving husband Michael, my children, Michael Jr., Kristie, Michele, Christopher, and Melodee.

To my father, Pastor Timothy Jenkins and each of my sisters, I say, "Forge on and fear not. God is with you all and will keep you from harm."

To the Williams Chapel Church family that I currently serve as Apostle and senior leader, I will always keep you lifted in my heart and prayers. You will do exploits as a people destined to reign. Thank you for praying for my strength in the Lord.

Introduction
Forgiveness and the Family

To Forgive Is to Live!
To Forgive Is to Heal!
To Release Is to Increase!

"Forgiveness does not change your past, but it does enlarge the future."–Paul Boese[1]

As I walk in solidarity with those who are trying to make sense of their struggles, unforgiveness seems to be a shackle and stronghold that positions itself against the healing of head and heart. For so many, life hurts and the hands that have inflicted wounds are hands initially experienced to be friendly and familiar. Wounded people wound others, even those they love. Unhealed hands that have held on to baggage and bitterness will only bind another to their skewed belief system.

---

[1] http://www.searchquotes.com/Paul_Boese/Forgiveness/quotes/

> "Grace empowers to forgive causing one to heal and ultimately live. He that forgives will continue to live fully and free." – David Augsburger[2]

Satan knows the power of unity and connectedness. He sets out to destroy peace and reconciliation leaving individuals wounded relationally. He knows that at the place of unity God commands the blessing. It is difficult to deal with the hurts that we don't deserve and yet remain in relationship with those who have inflicted the harm. David was a man who was wounded by those who should have encouraged him. He spoke to this in the Psalms.

> *For it was not an enemy that reproached me; then I could have borne it: neither was it he that hated me that did magnify himself against me; then I would have hid myself from him: But it was thou, a man mine equal, my guide, and mine acquaintance. We took sweet counsel together, and walked unto the house of God in company.* (Psalms 55:14)

Family can sometimes be the crucible whereby one is tested and refined. Crucibles facilitate a process that purges away impurities and creates a qualitatively different final product. The "fiery crucible" metaphor means a severe test or trial that refines and purifies. There will always be pain in a process of purification in the life of a believer.

Since family are those that are closest to us, it is there that we often face our greatest challenge with forgiveness. It is within the family unit that we are given the greatest opportunity to release those who have wounded us

---

[2] David Augsburger entitled; "The New Freedom of Forgiveness" 2000; Moody Press.

deeply, sometimes unjustly, sometimes unknowingly. We do this when we refuse to jeopardize our family relationships to hold onto unforgiveness.

We desire to be forgiven when we make a mistake, but find it hard to forgive others when they wound or betray us. We may even feel we are justified in our unforgiveness. Though forgiveness should be at the heart of our Christian walk, it is definitely easier said than done. In fact, it has been said that unforgiveness has become the cancer of Christianity. It is only through godly alignment that we can we walk in forgiveness.

To Release Is to Increase!

Godly Alignment

God knew exactly which family to place you and I in. He had a plan and fashioned our future story before we entered this world. Only the Lord knows what He has fully fashioned for our future. We must seek His face if we are to be fully aligned with His will.

Alignment is divine placement in the sphere God puts us in or calls us to in Him, to accomplish an assigned purpose and determined destiny. It is the place of peace even in pain. It is the place of completion before manifestation. Only a creator can call its creation to formation and fullness.

> *According as he hath chosen us in him before the foundation of the world, that we should be holy and without blame before him in love: Having predestinated us unto the adoption of children by Jesus Christ to himself, according to the good pleasure of his will, to the praise of the glory of his*

*grace, wherein **he hath made us accepted in the beloved.*** (Ephesians 1:4-6 emphasis added)

GOD DESIRES TO ALIGN OUR HEARTS WITH HIS IN ORDER FOR FORGIVENESS TO FLOW FREELY.

There are many examples within the Scriptures that lift before us the issue of forgiveness. Joseph gives us a clear view of the forgiveness challenge within the family. He experienced the vices of jealousy and envy among his siblings and yet he emerged with a forgiving heart. He understood that what Satan meant for evil, God used for good. Joseph was chosen by God and went from the pit to prison and ultimately to the palace.

Joseph was rejected by his brothers but accepted by God. As a matter of fact, I would go so far as to say that God preordained that Joseph would be rejected by those he loved. This would increase his capacity to love others and to be positioned in divine purpose and destiny.

> *My son, give me thine heart, and let thine eyes observe my ways.* (Proverbs 23:26)

> *Keep thy heart with all diligence; for out of it are the issues of life.* (Proverbs 4:23)

TO FORGIVE IS TO LIVE!

A healthy family is one that actively and responsibly addresses anything that seeks to cause a disruption, trouble or dysfunction in their relationships. Every family will know trouble, disruption, and dysfunction. However, wounds and pain become openings or occasions for growth and empowerment if dealt with through the power of God's love and Jesus' example of forgiveness.

LOVE IS PURIFIED IN PAIN WHILE THE CURE FOR PAIN IS ALWAYS IN THE PAIN.

> "Many people ruin their health and their lives by taking the poison of bitterness, resentment, and unforgiveness."
> – Joyce Meyer[3]

Unforgiveness can cause a shut down within one's soul. It is a dark and destructive vice that carries a lethal toxin. Unforgiveness will grip a heart and become infectious. It can travel through one's soul just as if it were a virus. It will try to justify its presence and will seek a long stay. The Bible gives us an example of this in the life of Absalom, David's son. The choices he made affected his whole family and his unforgiveness led him to commit horrendous crimes even within his own family.

The only cure for unforgiveness is the power of God's redemptive love expressed through the cross and applied to a human heart. Before the cross, we were taught to forgive to be forgiven, after the cross we know we are to forgive because we have been forgiven.

> *To whom ye forgive anything, I forgive also: for if I forgave anything, to whom I forgave it, for your sakes forgave*

---

[3] http://www.joycemeyer.org/Articles/ea.aspx?article=the_poison_of_unforgiveness

I it in the person of Christ; Lest Satan should get an advantage of us: for we are not ignorant of his devices. (2 Corinthians 2:10-11)

In order to remain in a relationship that is healthy, whenever an offense takes place, forgiveness is required. The difficult part is that forgiveness must be embraced regardless of whether the offender repents for his or her wrong doing. If we choose to carry unforgiveness around until we feel they deserve our forgiveness, we run the risk of being bound by a stronghold. This stronghold will set up its camp within our hearts and will affect our decisions and actions.

"When we forgive evil we do not excuse it, we do not tolerate it, we do not smother it. We look the evil full in the face, call it what it is, let its horror shock and stun and enrage us, and only then do we forgive it."–Lewis B. Smedes[4]

Defining Moments

Come now, and let us reason together, saith the Lord: though your sins be as scarlet, they shall be as white as snow; though they be red like crimson, they shall be as wool. (Isaiah 1:18)

Our adversary, Satan, desires for us to be relationally impaired, he hates unity and connectedness and will go to great lengths to sow discord

---

[4] http://www.goodreads.com/author/quotes/56576.Lewis_B_Smedes

and division. However, he does not hold the decision making power in a believer's life. Forgiveness is a choice. We must actively choose to forgive.

The battle is in the mind, but the victory has already been won in the spirit realm at Calvary. It is the Holy Spirit of promise that will lead us into all truth. God has equipped every believer with an overcoming power to tread upon the tactics and strategies of the enemy. We have the deciding vote. We have the power to overcome.

> "To forgive is to set a prisoner free and discover that the prisoner was you." – Lewis B. Smedes[5]

We are called to walk in the light of love and lay aside every weight and sin that can beset and hinder us from moving forward in life. Unforgiveness is a stronghold that will strangle our joy and leave us limping in this life and keep us from fully achieving all that God has called us to do.

A defining season is a season where divine momentum appears to be at a standstill. You're aware of and eagerly await the many prophetic promises God has spoken over your life. However, as you anticipate their arrival, you find yourself battling internally with living free from unforgiveness in your relationships.

Are you in a defining season?

If you are, submit your heart to God and evil will have to depart (James 4:7). Come with me as we free ourselves of any entanglements or generational baggage that has held our hearts captive to unforgiveness. At

---

[5] http://www.goodreads.com/author/quotes/56576.Lewis_B_Smedes

the cross, Jesus spoke forgiveness over those who sought His destruction and demise leaving us a godly example of what forgiveness is all about.

> *And when they were come to the place, which is called Calvary, there they crucified him, and the malefactors, one on the right hand, and the other on the left. Then said Jesus,* **Father, forgive them; for they know not what they do.** *And they parted his raiment, and cast lots.* (Luke 23:33-34 emphasis added)

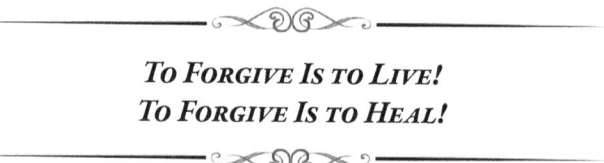

To Forgive Is to Live!
To Forgive Is to Heal!

I pray that as you read these pages, you will allow the Holy Spirit to minister to your mind, body, and soul. As you journey through the process of healing, ask Him to reveal to you where those strongholds of unforgiveness have gained access to your life.

Is there someone that you need to release in order to set yourself free?
Is there a hurt down deep that you haven't allowed to heal?
Is there unforgiveness causing you to distance yourself from a family member?

God desires to heal us down deep where the pain pulsates. Forgiveness is the process whereby we submit to God's purpose and His way. God's divine power has given us everything we need to live a life of godliness. His power enables us to escape the destruction the enemy seeks to cause in our lives and our families through unforgiveness. The enemy seeks to make us ineffective and unproductive. However, Jesus came to set the captives free from the bondage of unforgiveness and lead us into the abundant life. Abundant life will bring healing to our hearts and those we are called to serve.

> *My little children, these things write I unto you, that ye sin not. And if any man sin, we have an advocate with the Father, Jesus Christ the righteous: And he is the propitiation for our sins: and not for ours only, but also for the sins of the whole world.* (1 John 2:1-2)

TO FORGIVE IS TO LIVE!
TO FORGIVE IS TO HEAL!
TO FORGIVE IS TO INCREASE!

Chapter One

Uprooting the Root of Bitterness

Follow peace with all men, and holiness, without which no man shall see the Lord: Looking diligently lest-any man fail of the grace of God; lest any root of bitterness springing up trouble you, and thereby many be defiled. (Hebrews 12:14-15)

As a child, I spent countless hours with my maternal grandmother, Mattie Mae Anderson. She was a strong willed woman who knew the Lord and everyone else's business as well. If you disagreed with her, you dared not say so. She was a joy to live with and always told me stories about the family that I thought I knew, but she always seemed to know more, or so she thought.

I enjoyed the extra spin she seemed to add to the story with all of her passion and animation. My grandma, as I referred to her, would stand flat-footed and declare that the Lord didn't allow anything to escape her knowing. This always seemed a bit contradictory because my cousins and I engaged in some devious little things while she napped that God hadn't seemed to reveal to her. However, I certainly was not going to refute grandma's revelations. No one had survived refuting Mattie Mae without being the recipient of her great wrath.

Grandma didn't talk much about our family, but she certainly gave her opinion about the neighboring families. She was familiar with the conversation of the community. She knew those who were related but were not in relationship. She knew who was legally married but living elsewhere. Grandma knew who was pregnant and who was no longer pregnant. She knew whose uncle was really their father and whose mother was really their auntie. She could go back several generations to substantiate her story.

However knowledgeable my grandmother was about everyone else in the community, there seems to have been a lack of ownership of issues that were close to home. Somehow she would manage to stop the story before it got to her house. As I look back, I realize that it is always easier to mention someone else's misery than it is to mention our own.

Grandma's real inner struggle was with Mrs. Mae who I thought my grandfather married after he divorced my Grandma. I was totally misinformed! One night while awaiting my nightly story, Grandma went to the uncharted, unspoken subject of Mrs. Mae.

I could tell from the tension in the air that I had better not ask any questions, but simply listen to Grandma's version of my grandfather and Mrs. Mae's mysterious marriage. My ears were ready to hear, since no one else had been given this exclusive glance into Grandma's stuff.

Grandma stated that she didn't know how granddaddy and Mrs. Mae were ever married because no one ever served her with any kind of divorce papers. It appeared, granddaddy and Mrs. Mae weren't really married. Perhaps that was why granddaddy still came to visit Grandma each week.

As the story unfolded, I suddenly understood why Grandma would never allow us to eat any of the cakes that Mrs. Mae would send by my granddaddy during his weekly visits. Though she would always receive them kindly, deep inside she was bitter and angry. As soon as my grandfather left, she would take those pound cakes out on the back porch and just leave them there daring any of us to touch them. I still have visions of those pound cakes in my mind sitting there just being wasted. I reasoned in my mind that if Mrs. Mae was trying to poison Grandma and we ate the cakes, it would be okay since they weren't meant to hurt us. Unfortunately, the bitterness of unforgiveness was what was poisoning my Grandma.

> "Forgiving does not erase the bitter past. A healed memory is not a deleted memory. Instead, forgiving what we cannot forget creates a new way to remember. We change the memory of our past into a hope for our future." – Lewis B. Smedes[6]

Infrastructure of the Family

There is much to be unpacked studying our family's past. As a child, I didn't understand that families sometimes padded the pain of the past to deal with the present. This seemed to produce a pseudo form of peace and balance. Many families need to be transformed, a changing of the infrastructure if you would, in order to be healthy enough to battle the forces aligned against its wellbeing. An infrastructure is a basic organizational structure that serves as a foundation for any type of organization. Unforgiveness creates cracks and weakens the infrastructure of the family making it much more difficult to withstand the storms of life.

Satan knows that God created marriage as a beautiful, living picture of Christ and the church. God designed both marriage and the family for

---

[6] http://www.goodreads.com/author/quotes/56576.Lewis_B_Smedes

our wellbeing and growth. Satan knows the value of the family and that it is the infrastructure of a good solid society. The family is the foundation of vibrant growing assemblies, and the future of God's work on earth. If Satan can be successful in tearing down the infrastructure of the family unit, then he will be successful in damaging what is dear to God's heart. This has been one of Satan's most aggressive tactics from the very start.

When God finished creating the first couple, He called what He made "very good." This man and woman were united in the holy bond of marriage before God. For the benefit of future generations, God explained, "Therefore a man shall leave his father and his mother and cleave to his wife, and they shall become one flesh" (Genesis 2:24). God requires the married couple to develop a level of separation from others and a commitment to each other, which will provide a stable foundation for the family unit.

So much is riding on the family that it has become a place of enormous conflict when the relationships between husband and wife, parents and children, and child to child are not in proper alignment with God's original design. Many Bible characters experienced great warring within their families after they allowed the stronghold of unforgiveness to infect and poison their closest personal relationships.

David had a family system that was infected with fractured relationships that were handed down from father to son. Sometimes we are faced with generational curses that need to be dealt with to stop the dysfunction from being passed down through our family lines. This is why digging into the roots of the family system will help bring healing and new life to family relationships.

Rebecca helped Jacob steal Esau's birth right because of favoritism. Their struggle actually began in the womb. Though their mother was well aware of this struggle, she did not work with their father to resolve the issues when these twins were young. This struggle created a rift in the family for many years. Like some families today, instead of dealing with the issues properly, they choose to cut off communication altogether and physically separate themselves from the family unit.

The family can be considered a type of a womb. We are to grow and develop within the womb of our family just like a fetus is to grow and develop in his or her mother's womb. Like a womb, the family unit was designed by God to be a safe place for this growth and development to occur. However, for some, the growth process has been aborted due to abuse and other traumatic experiences affecting and infecting relationships in multiple generations.

Satan's initial attack on the family occurred in Eden where the serpent worked his evil deception on Eve and destroyed the harmony of the first marriage. In listening to Satan and disobeying God, Adam and Eve plunged themselves, and all subsequent families, into slavery in the "kingdom of darkness." Satan's attack on the family has continued until today. There are signs of it all around us and many are not skilled in diabolical spiritual warfare.

> *Therefore, as through one man sin entered into world, and death through sin; and so death passed unto all men, for that all sinned: for until the law sin was in the world; but sin is not imputed when there is no law. Nevertheless death reigned from Adam until Moses even over them that had not sinned after the likeness of Adam's transgression, who is a figure of him that was to come. But not as the trespass, so also is the free gift. For if by the trespass of the one the many died, much more did the grace of God, and the gift by the grace of the one man, Jesus Christ, abound unto the many. And not as through one that sinned, so is the gift: for the*

judgment came of one unto condemnation, but the free gift came of many trespasses unto justification. For if, by the trespass of the one, death reigned through the one; much more shall they that receive the abundance of grace and of the gift of righteousness reign in life through the one, even Jesus Christ. So then as through one trespass the judgment came unto all men to condemnation; even so through one act of righteousness the free gift came unto all men to justification of life. For as through the one man's disobedience the many were made sinners, even so through the obedience of the one shall the many be made righteous. (Romans 5:12-19)

FORGIVENESS IS A SUPERNATURAL HEALING PROCESS HEALING THE INFECTION OF MISERY AND PAIN.

Underground Unforgiveness

Be ye angry, and sin not: let not the sun go down upon your wrath. (Ephesians 4:26)

Being stuck in unforgiveness can become a stronghold that ultimately produces bitterness and wrath. When one is able to release the dark disease of unforgiveness, there is an inner freedom found that faces forward in life. Forgiveness brings one closer to the passion of Calvary. Before Jesus completed His God given sacrificial assignment, He released those who craved His destruction and demise. The Lord desires for us to forgive as we have been forgiven.

When one is stuck in unforgiveness they are unable to move or proceed with God's purpose. They can easily become entangled with the mire of anger or fear that resides underneath unforgiveness. This mire of unforgiveness is seductive, causing us to sink into a ground that is sure to restrain. It can become entrapment and oppressive if left undiagnosed and untreated.

Many believers become stuck and immobile as a result of wounds that have not healed and are still tender to the touch and memory. Loneliness is often caused because we do not seek to make peace with unresolved issues of unforgiveness. Forgiveness is a movement that frees us if we are willing to let go and let God bring healing and resolution.

We cannot allow unforgiveness to go underground because it becomes buried alive. It is unresolved and yet still active. Many times it becomes lodged in the subconscious and can act out through our conscious when we least expect it. The unconscious can be a driving force in relationships. It is the presence of forces within that lie beyond consciousness and yet are actively at work within our life.

Have you ever reacted to a situation in a way that surprised even you? You wondered to yourself, *Where did that come from*? *Why did I say or do that*? It came from an unresolved issue in your subconscious that was triggered by something seemingly unrelated. Anger and bitterness that results from unforgiveness can stew just below the surface of your subconscious and explode without warning. Paul knew this struggle all too well. He knew that there were forces deep within that warred against the spirit of his mind.

> *For that which I do I allow not: for what I would, that do I not; but what I hate, that do I. If then I do that which I would not, I consent unto the law that it is good. Now then it is no more I that do it, but sin that dwelleth in me. For I know that in me (that is, in my flesh,) dwelleth no good thing: for to will is present with me; but how to perform that which is good I find not. For the good that I would I do not: but the evil which I would not, that I do. Now if I do that I would not, it is no more I that do it, but sin that dwelleth in me. I find then a law, that, when I would do good, evil is present with me. For I delight in the law of God after the inward man: But I see another law in my members, warring against the law of my mind, and bringing me into captivity to the law of sin which is in my members.* (Romans 7:15-23)

The unconscious self remembers everything we have been taught. It remembers every time we have been abused. It remembers every time our feelings have been hurt. It remembers every time we have felt shamed. Although we are not consciously aware of these feelings, experiences, and memories, we are still impacted by them. When we are stressed, when we are in crises, when we are threatened, and when life seems to be out of control, the unconscious feelings can quickly come into action.

> *Behold, thou desirest truth in the inward parts: and in the hidden part thou shalt make me to know wisdom.* (Psalm 51:6)

Consciousness is the way we think and believe from our experiences, knowledge of our own existence, conditions, sensations, mental operations, and acts. It is the reality or awareness of the world and the knowledge of right and wrong according to our belief system. The average person generally operates out of about 15 percent of their consciousness.

> *Behold, I go forward, but he is not there; and backward, but I cannot perceive him: On the left hand, where he doth work, but I cannot behold him: he hideth himself on the right hand, that I cannot see him: But he knoweth the way that I take: when he hath tried me, I shall come forth as gold. My foot hath held his steps, his way have I kept, and not declined. Neither have I gone back from the commandment of his lips; I have esteemed the words of his mouth more than my necessary food. But he is in one mind, and who can turn him? and what his soul desireth, even that he doeth. For he performeth the thing that is appointed for me: and many such things are with him.* (Job 23:8-14)

Paul also recognized that he was unaware of all that lurked within, but that the Holy Spirit sent by Jesus and the Father is aware and can inform our consciousness.

> *These things have I spoken unto you, being yet present with you. But the Comforter, which is the Holy Ghost, whom the Father will send in my name, he shall teach you all things, and bring all things to your remembrance, whatsoever I have said unto you.* (John 14:25-26)

Amnon, Tamar, and Absalom

Amnon was the half-brother of Absalom and Tamar. Amnon was vexed with a strong spirit of lust and cunningly raped his half-sister Tamar. Tamar was instructed by her brother Absalom to keep the abuse silent and secret. Deep inside Absalom would never forgive Amnon and would eventually kill him as a way of avenging Tamar's virginity and sexual violation.

Tamar went into what I would call a deep destructive silence and seclusion. After her innocence was forcibly taken from her, she wept from the devaluation she experienced from someone she thought she could trust.

When David hears of this incest within his family, he responds angrily. However, we are never told that he held anyone accountable for this incestuous crime. Absalom on the other hand took vengeance into his mind and upcoming mission and as a result, much evil came to the kingdom.

> *When King David heard what had happened, he was very angry. And though Absalom never spoke to Amnon about this, he hated Amnon deeply because of what he had done to his sister.* (2 Samuel 13:21-22 NLT)

As you read the sad account in 2 Samuel 13-18, note how many people were affected, infected, and hurt by this incest and abuse. On top of the wrong done to his sister Tamar, Absalom's anger affected his relationship with not only the offender, his brother Amnon, but all of his brothers. It adversely affected his relationship with his father David for many years and eventually even led to a conspiracy against his own father.

> *A messenger soon arrived in Jerusalem to tell David, "All Israel has joined Absalom in a conspiracy against you!"*

> *"Then we must flee at once, or it will be too late!" David urged his men. "Hurry! If we get out of the city before Absalom arrives, both we and the city of Jerusalem will be spared from disaster."* (2 Samuel 15:13-14 NLT)

The Family Systems Theory

The Family Systems Theory was introduced by Dr. Murray Bowen and suggests that individuals cannot be understood in isolation from one another, but rather as a part of their family emotional unit. When we are born into a family system, we are born into invisible dynamics that have been at work from generation to generation. A family system can pass on burdens, curses, belief systems, secrets, strengths, and unresolved issues. Edwin Friedman in his book entitled; *Generation to Generation,* says that every problem within a family can be traced back at least three generations.

The family is a social unit of people descended from a common ancestry. It is a system of interconnected and interdependent individuals. God fashions each family with sacred specific characteristics. Families must be founded on submission to God and to each other in order to function in a healthy manner.

Not one family in the Bible was free from painful struggle or hurt. God does not want us to live superficially with the pretense that our lives are okay. Centuries of family history recorded in the Bible reveal that biblical families faced the same issues families face today and would often deny their problems and their pain in the same ways. They pretended to live as if everything was okay even though there was alcoholism, marriages that lacked intimacy, sexual addiction, abuse, codependency, and even murder present within their families.

We have been introduced to individuals in the scriptures who were angry and full of wrath. These individuals were not willing to forgive or work towards reconciliation. Absalom was unwilling to release his anger through the grace of forgiveness. It resulted in bringing further pain, hurt, disgrace, discord, and destruction among his entire family unit.

BETRAYAL IS WHAT SOMEONE DOES TO YOU, BUT BITTERNESS IS WHAT YOU DO TO YOURSELF.

Looking diligently lest any man fail of the grace of God; lest any root of bitterness springing up trouble you, and thereby many be defiled. (Hebrews 12:15)

Uprooting the Root of Bitterness

One can be affected and not infected. What do you think is the difference? Affected is influenced or touched by an external factor, while infected is internally contaminated with a contagion. Harboring hurt feelings will cause the heart to house anger and eventually bitterness causing the person to be infected from the inside out. Eventually what is inside will become evident on the outside, first with words and then with actions. Jesus taught about this in Matthew 12:33-35.

> *"A tree is identified by its fruit. If a tree is good, its fruit will be good. If a tree is bad, its fruit will be bad. You brood of snakes! How could evil men like you speak what is good and right? For whatever is in your heart determines what you say. A good person produces good things from the treasury*

of a good heart, and an evil person produces evil things from the treasury of an evil heart." (NLT)

Bitterness is very much like the South American vine known as the "matador." Beginning at the foot of a tree, the matador vine slowly works its way to the top. As it grows, it kills the tree, and when at last the top is reached, it sends forth a flower to crown itself. The word Matador literally means "killer." Bitterness may appear harmless when it is small, but if it is allowed to grow, its tendrils of resentment, malice, and hatred soon clasp themselves around the heart and eventually infect the soil of the soul. If we allow bitterness to take root, it will eventually destroy us and even our closest relationships. Hebrews 12:15 says it not only troubles us personally, it can also defile and contaminate many of those around us.

In her book, "Beauty for Ashes," Joyce Meyer said, "First, let me say that it is not possible to have good emotional health while harboring bitterness, resentment, and unforgiveness. Harboring unforgiveness is like drinking poison and hoping your enemy will die! Unforgiveness poisons anyone who holds it, causing him to become bitter. It is impossible to be bitter and get better at the same time!"

It's time to ask yourself:

- *Am I continually thinking destructive thoughts about the person who has harmed me?*
- *Am I happy at that person's misfortune?*
- *Do I find myself thinking up scenarios about what I wish I could do or say to them?*
- *Do I find myself trying to turn others against this person?*

BITTERNESS IS A DEADLY PLAGUE THAT CAN DEVOUR YOUR DESTINY!
BITTERNESS MUST BE CUT OUT AND CUT OFF AT THE ROOT!
IT'S TIME TO BECOME BETTER AND GET RID OF BITTERNESS!

"Never succumb to the temptation of bitterness."–Martin Luther King, Jr.

Chapter 2

Seemingly Stuck

Asked by the Pharisees when the kingdom of God would come, He [Jesus] replied to them by saying, "The kingdom of God does not come with signs to be observed or with visible display, Nor will people say, Look! Here [it is]! or, See, [it is] there! For behold, the kingdom of God is within you [in your hearts] and among you [surrounding you]." (Luke 17:20-21 AMP)

There are situations and seasons of life that will mandate a **must move**. This movement is predicated on a defining moment and a once in a lifetime experience. It is pregnant with potential and possibilities that might not be popular. However, to maintain a healthy mindset, we "gotta" go!

G.O.T.T.A = Get Out This Time Around

If we refuse to move, we could get stuck in a place that will prevent us from receiving all that God had designed for us. The word **stuck** means to be fixed, immovable, and bogged down. The mindset of being stuck can cause us to miss a move that God is trying to manifest in our life. I have come to realize that the state of being stuck can be a learned behavior that is the continuation of a cycle. The inability to function and flow in the movement of life can sometimes be attributed to one's parental performance. All behavior is motivated and in most cases learned.

My mother was very meticulous about the house being clean and tidy when I was a young girl. She would often chastise my sisters and I when we failed to clean to her standards. Sometimes I would quickly clean so that I could go outside. I knew that if she inspected the area and it was not considered neat to her standards, she would redo it. I realized early in my parenting that I too would reprimand my children if they failed to pick up behind themselves. Often I would make an excuse to redo the cleaning.

There are times in life when one has to be intentional in breaking toxic unhealthy ways of thinking. It can be as simple as changing the company we keep. We can make the mistake of surrounding ourselves with individuals with like misery. Especially in this area of forgiveness, we often seek to hang around with those who agree with our reason for not extending forgiveness. However, it is to our advantage to navigate towards those who are where we want to go and will help us keep from getting stuck in unforgiveness.

It Is All About Mindset

Seemingly becoming stuck in unforgiveness is all about ones mindset. Our perception of our own ability and worth can keep us stuck in a grasshopper mentality. We can't think of ourselves as being incapable of greatness or unworthy of God's goodness. When Moses sent the spies into the Promised Land to spy out the land, ten of them sized themselves up based on the giants they saw. They reported back to Moses and the people saying, "We were as grasshoppers in our own eyes." They could not look through the eyes of faith and possibility.

They became stuck in their own perception and were unwilling to move into the supernatural ability of Jehovah. It caused them to become weak and they became as dead men to the move of God. The wilderness walk of forty years would be the extent of their future.

God has ordained new places for our feet to walk. He has assigned new chapters to our future story that are set to His timing. Being unwilling to change and/or shift with the seasons of God's choosing can be detrimental to one's destiny. Keeping an open willing mind can be the difference between life and death.

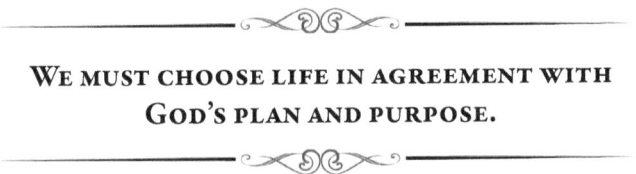

WE MUST CHOOSE LIFE IN AGREEMENT WITH GOD'S PLAN AND PURPOSE.

God's will is to perform His plan and purpose in and through us, therefore, we must be willing to go when He says go, stay when He says stay, and extend forgiveness even to those who have wounded us along the way. Failing to do so can not only affect our lives but those of future generations as well.

> *Wherein he hath abounded toward us in all wisdom and prudence; Having made known unto us the mystery of his will, according to his good pleasure which he hath purposed in himself.* (Ephesians 1:8-9)

> "The eyes of the future are looking back at us and they are praying for us to see beyond our own time." –Terry Tempest Williams

Timing Is Everything

In the New Testament, *kairos* time is the appointed time of the purpose of God; it is when God works. The Kingdom is already within us, but yet to come into fullness in our lives. Our prayer should continually be, "Thy kingdom come; thy will be done on earth as it is in heaven."

Time depicted in Greek is *kronos*, which is the general process of time chronologically measured by seconds, minutes, hours, weeks, months, and calendar. *Kairos* is the extension of *kronos* going beyond human calculation.

In timing, *kairos* portrays a seasonable time that is accompanied with "once in a lifetime opportunity." It is the "now" time! God interrupts silent seasons with *kairos* timing. *Kairos* time is a time in between, a moment of indeterminate time (not exactly known) in which something divinely appointed happens. *Kronos* is quantitative (measured by quantity) while *kairos* is qualitative (measured by quality). *Kairos* is a passing instant when an opening appears which must be driven through with force if manifested success is to be achieved.

We must seek to spiritually discern the ordered times of God. The men of Issachar were men who knew and understood the times (2 Chronicles 12:32). As the process of God's plan unfolds, *kronos* becomes *kairos*! *Kairos* is an opportunity to perform a task. It is a definitive moment that demands a response. *Kairos* is a time which requires a change or reorienting. It calls for action and transformation. If we are stuck in unforgiveness, we may not be able to discern the moment or be willing to do what is necessary to move into the new season God has prepared for us.

Tamar was deeply abused and hurt by someone she trusted. She was in desperate need of help to move forward after this devastating event. However, Absalom instructed Tamar not to move out of his house or interfere with the plans that he strategically devised for the demise of Amnon. As a result, Tamar remained desolate, stuck in Absalom's house. She was shackled with shame and unable to access the healing she needed to recover. She was isolated and had no one to release her from the dehumanizing grip of a wounding she did not deserve.

There are times in our lives when we try to defend our right to unforgiveness. The struggle is often about the fear of the consequences. However, remaining where we are will destroy our hope and our peace as we saw happen with Tamar.

I experienced a situation once where a husband married a second wife without divorcing the first wife. When the first wife found out, she felt betrayed, rejected, and abandoned by her husband. This experience caused the entire family to unravel. Initially, I felt that the wife had every right to be angry and emotionally closed. However, it wasn't long before I realized the anger was choking out her life.

> "Incubated hatred can elevate blood pressure, ulcerate a stomach, accelerate stress or invite a coronary." – David Augsburger[7]

Stuck in Unforgiveness

And do not grieve the Holy Spirit of God [do not offend or vex or sadden Him], by Whom you were sealed (marked,

---

[7] David Augsburger entitled; "The New Freedom of Forgiveness" 2000; Moody Press.

branded as God's own, secured) for the day of redemption (of final deliverance through Christ from evil and the consequences of sin). Let all bitterness and indignation and wrath (passion, rage, bad temper) and resentment (anger, animosity) and quarreling (brawling, clamor, contention) and slander (evil-speaking, abusive or blasphemous language) be banished from you, with all malice (spite, ill will, or baseness of any kind). And become useful and helpful and kind to one another, tenderhearted (compassionate, understanding, loving-hearted), forgiving one another [readily and freely], as God in Christ forgave you. (Ephesians 4:30-32 AMP)

Had Tamar received the right advice and counsel from her brother, she might have been able to move on with her life. If we are unable to forgive hurts, especially the ones we did not deserve, it can cause us to get stuck where we are and prevent us from receiving deliverance and peace. When we do not confront and care for the wound, our unforgiveness can become hatred that kills relationships and keeps us from moving forward toward fulfilling God's purpose in our lives.

The manifestations of unforgiveness are:

- Bitterness – bondage to dark inner hatred; internalized extreme intense hostility
- Wrath – a lethal lash that can sever the soul; a deep desire for revenge
- Anger – feeling threatened by a deep grievance of displeasure
- Clamor – shouting loudly, protesting, demanding
- Evil speaking – a release of words that have a destructive assignment

A spirit of unforgiveness develops when we choose to remain stuck in a state of unforgiveness toward a person who has wronged us. We know we are stuck in the spirit of unforgiveness when we say things like, "I don't think I can ever forgive that person or what they did to me."

Unforgiveness is a choice we make with our mind, will, and emotions. In order for us to be "well within," we must forgive from the will. Forgiveness can not be forced or demanded.

The Will

> *And I know that nothing good lives in me, that is, in my sinful nature. I want to do what is right, but I can't. I want to do what is good, but I don't. I don't want to do what is wrong, but I do it anyway. But if I do what I don't want to do, I am not really the one doing wrong; it is sin living in me that does it.* (Romans 7:18-20 NLT)

The mental faculty by which we deliberately choose or decide upon a course of action is the will. The will involves both desire and purpose. Desire is to strive to satisfy self and its appetite. Ultimately, the will has to be delivered and set free to forgive. Sometimes our will can't live up to what our mind and emotions feel and believe. Our mind knows and believes what is right while our emotions feel, but our will decides what we will or will not do. Our will is influenced by many outside agents all seeking to lead the will astray. The will can be fatally flawed because of our sin nature. A depraved mind without the Spirit's control results in a corrupted will. With the corrupted will we have inherited, it is impossible for man or woman to do what is right in the flesh without the leading of the Holy Spirit.

We must be intentional in releasing those we are holding in unforgiveness. The mind cannot control the will alone. There must be a fleeing from the influences that keep us stuck in unforgiveness and a running to the way, the truth, and the life through Christ. We cannot do it in our own strength, but Christ working in and through us can break us free from the self-imposed bondage of unforgiveness.

We must choose to forgive for the sake of our own mental, emotional, and physical health. Unforgiveness keeps us stuck in emotional bondage, damages relationships, blocks intimacy with God, and can even cause damage to the physical body. An unforgiving spirit is corruptive, destructive, and degenerative.

UNFORGIVENESS IS LIKE A SLOW POISON THAT WORKS IN THE SOUL, THE SPIRIT, AND EVEN THE BODY.

A Healthy Relationship Requires Much Work.

> *The Spirit of the LORD is upon me, for he has anointed me to bring Good News to the poor. He has sent me to proclaim that captives will be released, that the blind will see, that the oppressed will be set free.* (Luke 4:18 NLT)

Healing a relationship involves shared effort and risk. The cure for the pain is always found in the pain. Healing wounded relationships is a two-person job. Making a relationship work means deciding both people have real and positive options, and both committing to them. The individuals involved in a conflictual relationship must be willing to work at resolution and restoration.

You must have the same attitude that Christ Jesus had. Though he was God, he did not think of equality with God as something to cling to. Instead, he gave up his divine privileges; he took the humble position of a slave and was born as a human being. When he appeared in human form, he humbled himself in obedience to God and died a criminal's death on a cross. (Philippians 2:5-8 NLT)

God is relational, therefore, in our desire to be more Christ like, we face the challenge of becoming more "relationally competent." At the core of healing wounded relationships is the committed willingness to properly communicate and forgive. There is a surgery stage and then a recovery stage just like with a physical wounding. The surgery stage of relational healing is confession and apology which should happen as quickly as possible to avoid long term relational wounding. The more complex recovery stage of forgiveness that leads to true healing and restoration of the relationship takes more time.

The cause of the wounding often determines the length of the healing and restoration stage. Unrealistic expectations, infidelity, broken promises, and violated trust all require various recovery times. Give it time, healing is a process not an event and wounds of the heart heal slowly. Don't expect things to move back to normal right away. Remember, just like with a physical healing, people heal at different rates, especially when a person's trust has been violated. Intimacy is replaced by painful emotional and physical distance and healing will take time and hard work.

However, no matter what the cause, we cannot allow unforgiveness to lodge in our spirits. If we do, we will be stuck in unforgiveness and miss the blessings God has in place for us as we move into His plan and His purpose for our lives.

Defining Moments

There are situations and seasons of life that will mandate a **must move**. This movement is predicated on a **defining moment**. It is pregnant with potential and possibilities that might not be popular. However, to maintain a healthy mindset, you've "gotta" get unstuck!

G.O.T.T.A = Get Out This Time Around

It's Time to Ask Yourself:

Am I stuck in unforgiveness?
Why won't I release the accused?
Why am I denying forgiveness to this individual?
What do I see to be the greatest challenge to healing this wounded relationship?
Am I willing to get "unstuck" no matter what it takes?

Here is a quick checklist to help you begin the healing of a wounded relationship:

- Detect/discover the wound (violated trust, unrealistic expectations, infidelity, broken promises).
- Define the real root of the unforgiveness (fear, shame, justification, root of bitterness).
- Dialogue with the people involved and apologize for your part in the estranged relationship even if you were the one initially wronged.

- Decide to take the first step and offer forgiveness even if the other person is not repentant (cut bitterness off at the root).
- Design a plan of action to begin to rebuild trust within that relationship.
- Do whatever it takes on a consistent basis realizing the total healing may take time.

Chapter 3

Unforgiveness Blinds Vision

*So we don't look at the troubles we can see now; rather, **we fix our gaze on things that cannot be seen.** For the things we see now will soon be gone, but the things we cannot see will last forever.* (2 Corinthians 4:18 NLT emphasis added)

Seeing the Unseen

There are invisible forces at work in our lives and within our relationships that we are not always aware of. They are experiences that are buried deep within our subconscious waiting to emerge into our knowing. This scripture is very clear in speaking of the unseen and that which we see. We actually know in part and our thoughts are not necessarily God's thoughts.

> *For my thoughts are not your thoughts, neither are your ways my ways, saith the Lord. For as the heavens are higher than the earth, so are my ways higher than your ways, and my thoughts than your thoughts.* (Isaiah 55:8-9)

Our prayer must be to continuously seek the guidance and knowledge of God's leading. Our knowing is limited and is based on what we are conscious of. When we live only by what we can see, we are not controlled by truth, but by what we believe or perceive to be truth. It is not until we recognize our limited thinking that we are able to choose to alter it and move into our true destiny.

Sarah couldn't see the unseen when the angel spoke to her and informed her of the child that would come from her womb. She allowed her human inabilities to block her from seeing God's ability. She laughed at the prophetic promise that was pronounced over her destiny. She could not envision the vision of God. However, God remained faithful to His word.

> *And the Lord appeared unto him in the plains of Mamre: and he sat in the tent door in the heat of the day; And he lift up his eyes and looked, and, lo, three men stood by him: and when he saw them, he ran to meet them from the tent door, and bowed himself toward the ground, And said, My Lord, if now I have found favour in thy sight, pass not away, I pray thee, from thy servant: Let a little water, I pray you, be fetched, and wash your feet, and rest yourselves under the tree: And I will fetch a morsel of bread, and comfort ye your hearts; after that ye shall pass on: for therefore are ye come to your servant. And they said, So do, as thou hast said. And Abraham hastened into the tent unto Sarah, and said, Make ready quickly three measures of fine meal, knead it, and make cakes upon the hearth. And Abraham ran unto the herd, and fetched a calf tender and good, and gave it unto a young man; and he hasted to dress it. And he took*

butter, and milk, and the calf which he had dressed, and set it before them; and he stood by them under the tree, and they did eat. And they said unto him, Where is Sarah thy wife? And he said, Behold, in the tent. And he said, I will certainly return unto thee according to the time of life; and, lo, Sarah thy wife shall have a son. And Sarah heard it in the tent door, which was behind him. Now Abraham and Sarah were old and well stricken in age; and it ceased to be with Sarah after the manner of women. Therefore Sarah laughed within herself, saying, after I am waxed old shall I have pleasure, my lord being old also? (Genesis 18:1-12)

As I consider the family dynamics that manifested between Abraham, Sarah, and Hagar, I would imagine that Sarah really struggled with some issues of unforgiveness that paralyzed her perception of her future. Unforgiveness can paralyze one's ability to flow forward with an undivided heart. If the heart is divided, the mind cannot be aligned and decisions will not line up with God's perfect will.

Sarah's first struggle within her soul was her battle with her sense of self-worth and why she was barren in the midst of women who were giving birth continuously. Her jealousy, anger, and frustration festered while her past condition hindered her from embracing the present promise. She was blind to the fact that the favor God placed over her life preceded calculated human favor. She wanted to take the lead in her life and so made some poor decisions based on what she could see and not God's truth.

We must consider Sarah's laugh and its true meaning. Sarah lost a lot in that laugh. She lost her willingness to wait on God's promise and her ability to submit to God's appointed time. With those losses came many more monsters of the mind that refuted her faith.

As I consider Sarah's laugh, it was likely anchored in anger and disguised as sarcasm. The mask that she wore was to hide the deep entrenched misery she suffered. Sarah, in all of her natural beauty, could not produce the one thing that showered true beauty upon the integrity of women during her era of time. Her misery turned to anger and jealousy which led to almost missing God's promise.

> *But God hath chosen the foolish things of the world to confound the wise; and God hath chosen the weak things of the world to confound the things which are mighty; And base things of the world, and things which are despised, hath God chosen, yea, and things which are not, to bring to nought things that are.* (1 Corinthians 1:27-28)

Spiritual vision requires one to see beyond human sight to the preferred future that God has ordained for them. Unforgiveness will blur one's prophetic vision and in some instances, it will completely blind one's acute vision.

Jonah Blinded by Anger and Unforgiveness

> *Now the word of the Lord came unto Jonah the son of Amittai, saying, Arise, go to Ninevah, that great city, and cry against it; for their wickedness is come up before me. But Jonah rose up to flee unto Tarshish from the presence of the Lord, and went down to Joppa; and he found a ship going to Tarshish: so he paid the fare thereof, and went down into it, to go with them unto Tarshish from the presence of the Lord.* (Jonah 1:1-3)

Jonah is indicative of another believer who got stuck in a mindset that hindered him from becoming the change agent God intended him to be. He became entangled in the poison of his anger until he resisted God's clear instructions. He was so anchored in his anger and unforgiveness that his desire for the Ninevites to suffer kept him blinded to God's ultimate plan. He justified the poison deep within him and remained fixed in resistance to reconciliation.

> *But the Lord sent out a great wind into the sea, and there was a mighty tempest in the sea, so that the ship was like to be broken. Then the mariners were afraid, and cried every man unto his god, and cast forth the wares that were in the ship into the sea, to lighten it of them. But Jonah was gone down into the sides of the ship; and he lay, and was fast asleep. And they said everyone to his fellow, Come, and let us cast lots, that we may know for whose cause this evil is upon us. So they cast lots, and the lot fell upon Jonah. Then said they unto him, Tell us, we pray thee, for whose cause this evil is upon us; What is thine occupation? And whence comest thou? What is thy country? And of what people art thou? Then were the men exceedingly afraid, and said unto him, Why has thou done this? For the men knew that he fled from the presence of the Lord, because he had told them. So they took up Jonah, and cast him forth into the sea: and the sea ceased from her raging. Now the Lord had prepared a great fish to swallow up Jonah. And Jonah was in the belly of the fish three days and three nights.* (Jonah 1:4-5, 7-8, 10, 15, 17)

> *Then Jonah prayed unto the Lord his God out of the fish's belly, And said, I cried by reason of mine affliction unto the Lord, and he heard me; out of the belly of hell cried I, and thou heardest my voice. And the Lord spake unto the fish, and it vomited out Jonah upon the dry land.* (Jonah 2:1-2, 10)

Forgiveness would have freed Jonah from the bondage of judgment. He quickly forgot that the Lord had released him from his own debt of disobedience. It is easy to accept God's grace and forgiveness for ourselves, but quite another thing to extend it to others, especially those who have hurt us.

> *And the word of the Lord came unto Jonah the second time, saying, Arise, go unto Ninevah, that great city, and preach unto it the preaching that I bid thee. So Jonah arose, and went unto Nineveh, according to the word of the Lord. Now Ninevah was an exceeding great city of three days' journey. And Jonah began to enter into the city a day's journey, and he cried, and said, Yet forty days, and Ninevah shall be overthrown. So the people of Ninevah believed God, and proclaimed a fast, and put on sackcloth, from the greatest of them even to the least of them. And God saw their works, that they turned from their evil way; and God repented of the evil, that he had said that he would do unto them; and he did it not.* (Jonah 3:1-5, 10)

> *But it displeased Jonah exceedingly, and **he was very angry**. And he prayed unto the Lord, and said, I pray thee, O Lord, was not this my saying, when I was yet in my country?*

Therefore I fled before unto Tarshish: for I knew that thou art a gracious God, and merciful, slow to anger, and of great kindness, and repentest thee of the evil. Therefore now, O Lord, take, I beseech thee, my life from me; for it is better for me to die than to live. Then said the Lord, Doest thou well to be angry? So Jonah went out of the city, and sat on the east side of the city, and there made him a booth, and sat under it in the shadow, till he might see what would become of the city. And the Lord God prepared a gourd, and made it to come up over Jonah, that it might be a shadow over his head, to deliver him from his grief. So Jonah was exceeding glad of the gourd. But God prepared a worm when the morning rose the next day, and it smote the gourd that it withered. And it came to pass, when the sun did arise, that God prepared a vehement east wind; and the sun beat upon the head of Jonah, that he fainted, and wished in himself to die, and said, It is better for me to die than to live. And God said to Jonah, Doest though well to be angry for the gourd? And he said, I do well to be angry, even unto death. Then said the Lord, Thou hast had pity on the gourd, for the which thou hast not labored, neither madest it grow; which came up in a night, and perished in a night: And should not I spare Ninevah, that great city, wherein are more than sixscore (120,000) thousand persons that cannot discern between their right hand and their left hand; and also much cattle? (Jonah 4:1-11 emphasis added)

Jonah's disobedience was based on the fact that he foresaw that the Ninevites would repent and God would forgive them. He wanted God to withhold forgiveness from them. Ninevah was the capital of Assyria and Assyria had taken the northern kingdom into captivity and inflicted great harm on them. Jonah's disobedience was based on the fact that he foresaw that the Ninevites would repent and God would forgive them. He wanted to withhold forgiveness from them because of the hurt they had inflicted upon his people.

Jonah appears to be a very angry man unwilling to extend forgiveness to the Ninevites when God had forgiven him of his initial disobedience. Then when Jonah prayed to God from the fish's belly and repented of his evil, God heard him and released him from the belly of the fish. Jonah was familiar with this side of God. However, when God decided to extend this same mercy to the Ninevites, Jonah became so angry that he left the city, shut down, and began to entertain suicidal thoughts.

The Lord is longsuffering toward Jonah even in his resistance to release the Ninevites. Jonah is stuck in his unforgiveness and is unable to move any further in life. He is bogged down in the mire of anger and the quicksand of unforgiveness.

- His self-justified anger is resistant to the loving voice of God.
- He is displeased with God's forgiveness of his enemies.
- His anger displaces his desire to live.
- He dislodges and distances himself from life and does not respond to God.
- Jonah watched the city with hopes it would turn out "his way."
- He refused to accept God's forgiveness of Nineveh.
- Defiant grief gained momentum in Jonah's spirit to the point he mourns the mercy of God toward Nineveh.

**TO FORGIVE IS TO SET A PRISONER FREE AND
THEN YOU MAY DISCOVER THE PRISONER WAS YOU.
UNFORGIVENESS IS LIKE DRINKING POISON AND
WAITING FOR SOMEONE ELSE TO DIE.**

We are left without knowing if Jonah ever chooses deliverance by accepting God's reasoning. We actually get to decide the outcome in our own lives. We need to allow Jonah's experience to help us choose wisely.

The Chief Liberator

> *The Spirit of the LORD is upon me, for he has anointed me to bring Good News to the poor. He has sent me to proclaim that captives will be released, that the blind will see, that the oppressed will be set free.* (Luke 4:18 NLT)

There is a liberating call resounding within the hearts of man. It is a call to freedom in the fullest sense. Jesus came to set the captives free. He came that you and I might walk in the fullness of grace and truth. Liberation is the prophetic response to oppression. The kingdom of God is at hand and we must prepare the way of the Lord and fulfill the call He has given us.

> *And we believers also groan, even though we have the Holy Spirit within us as a foretaste of future glory, for we long for our bodies to be released from sin and suffering. We, too, wait with eager hope for the day when God will give us our full rights as his adopted children, including the new bodies he has promised us.* (Romans 8:23 NLT)

The living God is not a God of entrapment, but a God of empowerment. The God of scripture is not a God of limitation, but a God of liberation. He is not a God who holds back, but a God who sets us free.

The Holy Spirit is moving in such a way that there is a deep inner groan within the soul of many that is waiting for release. We must take up our bed, pick up the very thing that has held us down, bound us, disabled us, and forced us to live on the edge of God's will. We must refuse to allow it to keep us stuck in the quicksand of unforgiveness.

Like Jonah, much of our inner battle is connected to our deepest fear. Yes, the struggle is strong, but God is stronger. We must proclaim the release to the captives and recovering of sight to those who refuse to look on the Savior and live.

> *Even as David also describeth the blessedness of the man, unto whom God imputeth righteousness without works, Saying, Blessed are they whose iniquities are forgiven, and whose sins are covered. Blessed is the man to whom the Lord will not impute sin.* (Romans 4:6-8)

We receive God's forgiveness the moment we were enabled of the Holy Spirit to trust Christ as our Savior from sin. Our forgiveness is complete because of our justification in Christ, by which God declared us righteous in His Son. Before the cross, the Bible says we forgive to be forgiven. After the cross, Scripture teaches that we forgive because we have been forgiven. Jonah received God's forgiveness, but did not want God to extend it to his enemies. His anger blinded him to what God had called him to do and kept him stuck in the quicksand of unforgiveness.

Freed from the Quicksand of Unforgiveness

As I write today, I am reflecting on the past few months in which I was presented with some painful experiences that allowed past hurts to pulsate once again into my consciousness. I recognized the goodness of God's grace and its power to produce a process of forgiveness that was still underway.

What I quickly realized was that the misery in my memories had lessened and there was no longer a dark grip on my spirit. Though thoughts still presented themselves, they left as quickly as they came. There was no room for them to take up residence in my soul. The floors in my mind had been swept and were now occupied with furniture of a liberated life that had been freed from the quicksand of unforgiveness. This enabled me to pray without ceasing until I discovered my balance again.

One thing I knew for sure was that I was no longer bound by baggage from that particular hurt. I actually had the power to speak truth and stand upon its foundation. I was able to radically release my accused and consider them forgiven and free from condemnation.

As I move forward, I am at a season that feels like a second call. My initial call to ministry came at the age of sixteen and I am currently fifty-five. The years in between have been engaging and adventurous. I have been enlarged and my mindset has been expanded to see God in fresh new paradigms and expressions of love and grace.

I am convinced that God is designing a pattern on the canvas of my life. There are intricate pieces that connect and fit together to create a masterpiece of His choosing. There are times when His hands seem to be cutting, chiseling, pruning, and molding me for what appears to be a mission impossible. However, where He leads, I will follow. Even when I can't see the unseen, I know that He has already viewed the end state and will get me to my destiny.

> *The word which came to Jeremiah from the Lord, saying, Arise, and go down to the potter's house, and there I will cause thee to hear my words. Then I went down to the potter's house, and, behold, he wrought a work on the wheels. And the vessel that he made of clay was marred in the hand of the potter: so he made it again another vessel, as seemed good to the potter to make it. Then the word of the Lord came to me, saying, O house of Israel, cannot I do with you as this potter? saith the Lord. Behold, as the clay is in the potter's hand, so are ye in mine hand, O house of Israel. (Jeremiah 18:1-6)*

Defining Moments

There are times when God's hands seem to be cutting, chiseling, pruning, and molding me for a mission impossible. I have determined in my life that where He leads, I will follow. Even when I can't see the unseen, I know that He has already viewed the end state and will get me to my destiny. You can be assured of that same thing.

It's Time to Ask Yourself:

Will I determine to allow God to free me from the quicksand of unforgiveness?
Will I accept forgiveness for myself and for my enemies as well?
Will I allow God to cut, chisel, prune, and mold me for His mission for my life?
Will I follow where He leads even if it is to my own Ninevah?
Will I trust Him to get me to my true destiny even if it seems like mission impossible?

Chapter 4

Padded Pain

*At that moment their eyes were opened, and they suddenly felt shame at their nakedness. So they sewed fig leaves together **to cover themselves**. When the cool evening breezes were blowing, the man and his wife heard the Lord God walking about in the garden. So **they hid from the Lord God** among the trees.* (Genesis 3:7-8 NLT emphasis added)

Who wants to be seen for who they think they are? Ask Adam and Eve.

Made in the very image of God, Adam and Eve were fearfully and wonderfully made. However, once sin entered into their hearts, their inner sense of self became depraved. Their divine design would no longer be seen as pure. The fear and shame they now felt compelled them to cover what God had intricately and lovingly designed to be pure and admired. Their sense of self was covered with fig leaves that felt safe and more presentable to the natural eye. They no longer possessed a supernatural view of themselves, each other, or their future.

David's daughter, Tamar also experienced the marring of a masterpiece. Tamar was a virgin and wore a beautiful coat that was reserved for virgins only. After her innocence was taken from her, she tore her coat and wept from the devaluation she experienced from her brother. After Amnon raped her, her sense of self-worth died and that death took away her dignity and her desire to be seen or heard. Her beauty and her value were ripped from her reality.

In some cases, we might be tempted to cover or pad our pain with silence, anger, fear, bitterness, eating, shopping, addictions, as well as unforgiveness. However, at some point, the padding wears down and the intensity of the pain returns with a vengeance.

There is always a temptation to try to escape pain and hurt while navigating through relationships. This often proves to be utterly impossible when growth requires that we confront our pain if it is to ever be healed. Padding our pain fosters a sense of hiding our true self from ourselves, from others, and even from God. Whenever we experience hurt and abuse, there is a tendency to shield our heart against the possibility of future hurt. We often say; "No one will ever hurt me like that again."

A "pad" is defined as a material used to protect or comfort something. A pad could also be considered as a mindset used as a defense mechanism to foster denial. When padding is used within a mindset of denial, there is much activity floating around in the subconscious just waiting to surface at any given moment. We walk around like a ticking time bomb that could be exploded at any moment.

God cannot heal what we are unwilling to reveal to ourselves about ourselves. The truth is always present within the heart of God, so He waits for our arrival at a place called "submission." Submission sets a struggling soul free to become God's vessel of honor. Satan can never enter submission. The Bible tells us that if we submit ourselves to the Lord, then we will be able to resist Satan. Resisting Satan always rests upon our ability to rest in the power and provision of God.

Our challenge is to behold ourselves as Christ does. We are created in the very image of God. We are His workmanship created in Christ Jesus. We can only do this when we are willing to remove the protective padding we have wrapped ourselves in and open ourselves up to the healing power of our loving heavenly Father.

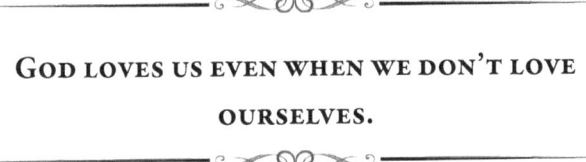

GOD LOVES US EVEN WHEN WE DON'T LOVE OURSELVES.

For now we are looking in a mirror that gives only a dim (blurred) reflection [of reality as in a riddle or enigma], but then [when perfection comes] we shall see in reality and face to face! Now I know in part (imperfectly), but then I shall know and understand fully and clearly, even in the same manner as I have been fully and clearly known and understood [by God]. (1 Corinthians 13:12 AMP)

Pain can become a place of growth and expansion in the life of a believer. David said, "It is good for me that I have been afflicted; that I might learn thy statutes." The Lord will always redeem the suffering of His children if we will submit to His ways and His timing in our lives. God's ways are higher than our ways and always with the purpose of moving us forward toward our true destiny.

> *When Job prayed for his friends, the L*ORD *restored his fortunes.* ***In fact, the L*ORD *gave him twice as much as before!*** *Then all his brothers, sisters, and former friends came and feasted with him in his home. And they consoled him and comforted him because of all the trials the L*ORD *had brought against him. And each of them brought him a gift of money and a gold ring.* ***So the L*ORD *blessed Job in the second half of his life even more than in the beginning.*** (Job 42:10-12 NLT emphasis added)

By the grace of God, we can place our padded pain in the hand of God for divine healing. Divine healing is always supernatural and usually takes on a form that is not recognizable with the human eye or with human reasoning.

Divine healing is the direct supernatural intervening act of the Holy Spirit, by which the body, spirit, and the soul are delivered from malady, disease, sickness, death, bondage, oppression (prolonged cruel control), and captivity. It is being restored to soundness of health in the whole man.

The supernatural takes place when God, through His Word and by His Spirit, steps into the natural. The term supernatural speaks of power that is not natural, but above and beyond the natural. Supernatural means it's higher, superior, and above the natural realm of existence.

The supernatural has authority over all things that are under the natural laws that God the creator of the heavens and the earth has put in place. Therefore, I can conclude that the supernatural rules over the earth. Everything under the sun is controlled and determined by the supernatural. When the supernatural is manifested it cannot be explained by any known natural law. The power of God's love can move our protective pads and place us in a place of transparency. However, God will not intervene and deliver our supernatural healing unless we ask Him for it.

I can remember when I was pregnant with my first child Michael Jr. The initial conception seemed to be with much risk. I can recall the doctor informing me that I should go home and stay in bed and prepare for the worst. He tried to alert me that I would probably lose the baby within seventy-two hours.

I, however, knew the Lord was a healer and could heal my body as well as strengthen my womb to carry my child to term. I cried out unto the Lord and asked Him to deliver me from the struggle. Later that night, I had a supernatural encounter that increased my faith capacity. As I slept, a small angelic little boy entered my room and placed his hand upon my stomach. He informed me that I was healed and that I would have a male child. I believed and received the blessing of my son at the appointed time.

THE CHALLENGE ENCOUNTERED BY MANY IS TO ANSWER JESUS' QUESTION, "DO YOU REALLY WANT TO BE MADE WHOLE AND WELL?" (JOHN 5:6)

Surviving a Season of Suffering

*In the days of His flesh [Jesus] offered up definite, special petitions [for that which He not only wanted but needed] and supplications with strong crying and tears to Him Who was [always] able to save Him [out] from death, and He was heard because of His reverence toward God [His godly fear, His piety, in that He shrank from the horrors of separation from the bright presence of the Father]. **Although***

> *He was a Son, He learned [active, special] obedience through what He suffered and, [His completed experience] making Him perfectly [equipped],* He became the Author and Source of eternal salvation to all those who give heed and obey Him, being designated and recognized and saluted by God as High Priest after the order (with the rank) of Melchizedek. (Hebrews 5:7-10 AMP emphasis added)

The next challenge is to answer the question, "Do you trust God with your future?" Jesus did. Although He was God's Son, He learned active obedience through what He suffered. Not only that, it perfectly equipped Him to become what God had called Him to be and to complete His mission. He not only survived, He was victorious over His afflictions. He was able to endure the humiliation and physical torment because He knew it was limited to a fixed span of time. He trusted God the Father to take Him all the way through to the destiny He was meant to fulfill.

The Bible also says, "This High Priest of ours understands our weaknesses, for he faced all of the same testings we do, yet he did not sin" (Hebrews 4:15 NLT). He suffered pain of the body, grief of the mind, and emotional injustice. There are numerous synonyms in Scripture for the word suffering such as affliction, anguish, distress, grief, misery, oppression, vexation, sorrow, travail, pain, tribulation, plague, chastisement, discipline, persecution, endurance, and woe.

Padded Pain

THERE ARE MANY ADVANTAGES TO BEING A CHRISTIAN, BUT THE ABSENCE OF PAIN IS NOT ONE OF THEM. PAIN IS A CRUCIBLE WHEREBY ONE LEARNS OBEDIENCE – JESUS DID!

However, painful experiences can haunt us, especially when we seek to pad and protect ourselves by denying the presence of our pain and refusing to confront the unforgiveness in our heart. Pain can cause us to place God's purpose for our lives on the back burner. Pain can also force a door open into the deep parts of our soul exposing that which we'd rather not admit.

It's how we handle our pain that matters. Does it position us before God or does it paralyze us with fear and anger that distance us from God?

> *"My servant Job will pray for you, and I will accept his prayer on your behalf. I will not treat you as you deserve, for you have not spoken accurately about me, as my servant Job has."*
> (Job 42:8 NLT)

Pain is undue pressure on the soul with an intensity designed to change who we are into who we are meant to become. It is a state of disorientation divinely designed with a plan to get us to our divine destiny.

So how do we survive our individual season of suffering and come out on the other side of victory like Job and Jesus did?

Surviving Our Season of Suffering

> *[But what of that?] For I consider that **the sufferings of this present time (this present life) are not worth being compared with the glory** that is about to be revealed to us and in us and for us and conferred on us!* (Romans 8:18 AMP emphasis added)

God never tells us to do something without giving us what we need to accomplish it. He has left us examples to teach us how to do things His way, in His timing, and that will bring us to His desired outcome for us.

Submit to God – Trust Him with your life and your future. Surrender your need, even in the area of forgiveness. The apostle Paul says, "And this is why I am suffering as I do. Still I am not ashamed, for I know (perceive, have knowledge of, and am acquainted with) Him Whom I have believed (adhered to and trusted in and relied on), and I am [positively] persuaded that He is able to guard *and* keep that which has been entrusted to me *and* which I have committed [to Him] until that day" (2 Timothy 1:12 AMP). God knows the end from the beginning and you can trust Him to bring you to His desired end.

Set Your Affections Above – Set your mind, position it in a steadfast place on the things of God and not on what you are currently going through. Mind the things which are above. Affection to the one will weaken and abate (diminish) affection to the other. The more you set your mind on the things of God, the less you will be tempted to focus on the things of the world. What you think about the most is what you will become. "And set your minds *and* keep them set on what is above (the higher things), not on the things that are on the earth" (Colossians 3:2).

Seize Control of the Soul – Jesus said, "By your steadfastness and patient endurance you shall win the true life of your souls" (Luke 21:19 AMP). Your soul is your mind, will, and emotions. Transformation is accomplished through the renewing of your mind (Romans 12:1-2). Only then can you behead belief systems that try to hold you in bondage and try to separate you from fulfilling your God-given purpose.

> *Who shall separate us from the love of Christ? Shall tribulation, or distress, or persecution, or famine, or nakedness, or peril, or sword? For I am persuaded, that neither death, nor life, nor angels, nor principalities, nor powers, nor things present, nor things to come, nor height, nor depth, nor any other creature, shall be able to separate us from the love of God, which is in Christ Jesus our Lord.* (Romans 8:35, 38-39)

Healing of head and heart are necessary because what settles in your head ultimately seizes your heart. Many are trying to numb the pain by staying stuck in the same place, doing the same thing, and holding onto the same unforgiveness. Padding our pain keeps God's healing power out and the destructive thoughts in.

> *Keep and guard your heart with all vigilance and above all that you guard, for out of it flow the springs of life.* (Proverbs 4:23 AMP)

One of the greatest things God uses to get us to move forward is pain. Pain is a signal that something is wrong and action is required. There is a difference between pain with a purpose and pain that's going nowhere. Pain should drive you to do something appropriate to end it. Some are stuck with chronic aches that have started to feel like their new normal, often believing the cure is worse than the disease. Fear of change leads us to pad the pain instead of confronting and seeking to remove what is causing it.

> "We change our behavior when the pain of staying the same becomes greater than the pain of changing. Consequences give us the pain that motivates us to change." – Henry Cloud

There are mindsets, people, addictions, jobs, and plans we have to give up in order to **move forward**. Today may be your enemy of your tomorrow if you are not willing to take the risk and change what needs to be changed. The tomorrow that you desire and envision may never come to pass if you do not end some things you are doing today. It's hard to be content in pain. Pain is designed to make you uncomfortable enough to want to change what God says needs to be changed.

> "C. S. Lewis said that God whispers through pleasure but shouts through pain. Sometimes our Father has to shout."
> – Bruce H. Wilkinson, "Secrets of the Vine: Breaking Through to Abundance"

Many try to self-medicate the pain by padding it and staying the same. The pain of staying the same and the fear of change are in constant conflict. This dual war will encourage you to stay in abusive relationships, keep drinking, keep cheating on your spouse, and hurting the very ones you love. You get to decide what the outcome will be. Change cannot happen until you make the choice to release what God tells you to give up and remove the protective padding you have hidden behind for too long.

In order for God to heal your head and your heart, you must be willing to allow the Holy Spirit to:

- Reposition your heart.
- Redirect your mind.
- Release God's renovation in your life.

PAIN IS NOT INTENDED FOR PUNISHMENT WHEN GOD IS ALLOWING IT. FOR THE CHILD OF GOD, PAIN HAS A PURPOSE. ASK JABEZ AND JOB.

Jabez was honorable above his brothers; ***but his mother named him Jabez [sorrow maker],*** *saying, Because I bore him in pain. Jabez cried to the God of Israel, saying, Oh, that You would bless me and enlarge my border, and that Your hand might be with me, and You would keep me from evil so it might not hurt me! And God granted his request.* (1 Chronicles 4:9-10 NLT)

Jabez was birthed in pain and his initial identity was marked by pain, but he cried unto the Lord. Talk about a generational curse! His own mother named him "pain." However, Jabez refused to pad his pain and remain stuck in an unproductive life. He trusted God and knew the way to victory was moving forward with God as His guide.

"Attempt something large enough that failure is guaranteed...unless God steps in!" from The Prayer of Jabez by Bruce Wilkinson

> *Then his wife said to him, Do you still hold fast your blameless uprightness? Renounce God and die! But he said to her, You speak as one of the impious and foolish women would speak. What? Shall we accept [only] good at the hand of God and shall we not accept [also] misfortune and what is of a bad nature? In [spite of] all this, Job did not sin with his lips.* (Job 2:9-10 AMP)

God will allow pain if it leads to our deliverance and healing. God never intends pain as a punishment but a warning sign. Though Job's friends told him God was punishing him for some sin in his life, Job knew God had a plan that had not yet been revealed to him. Pain can sometimes be a God thing which He allows for our ultimate good. We need to trust God, remove the pad from around our pain, and allow His divine healing all the way into our hearts and minds.

> *My suffering was good for me, for it taught me to pay attention to [God's] decrees.* (Psalm 119:71 AMP)

Defining Moments

The challenge encountered by many is to answer Jesus' question, "Do you really want to be made whole and well?" (John 5:6)

You get to choose. If your answer is, "Yes, I really do want to be made whole and well," then here is your "to do" list:

1. **Submit to God** – Remove the pad and trust Him with your life and your future.

2. **Set Your Affections Above**– Remove the pad and set your mind on His way and His timing. Position it in a steadfast place on the things of God and not on what you are currently going through.
3. **Seize Control of the Soul** – Jesus said, "By your steadfastness *and* patient endurance you shall win the true life of your souls" (Luke 21:19). Your soul is your mind, will, and emotions. Transformation is accomplished through the renewing of your mind (Romans 12:1-2).

Only then can you behead belief systems that try to hold you in bondage to unforgiveness. This can only be accomplished by removing the padding and being willing to change what God says need changing.

> *No discipline is enjoyable while it is happening—it's painful!* ***But afterward there will be a peaceful harvest of right living for those who are trained in this way.*** (Hebrews 12:11 NLT emphasis added)

It's Time to Ask Yourself:

> *Do I understand that pain presses out God's purpose in my life?*
>
> *Can I see that it is ultimately for my own good and not for punishment?*
>
> *Can I say with Psalm 119:71, "My suffering was good for me, for it taught me to pay attention to [God's] decrees" (AMP)?*

"What percentage of Christians do you think have experienced scourging? It may shock you to read that God scourges every son." – Bruce H. Wilkinson, "Secrets of the Vine: Breaking Through to Abundance"

Chapter 5

Basis for Forgiveness

Christ Took Our Punishment

But now God has shown us a way to be made right with him without keeping the requirements of the law, as was promised in the writings of Moses and the prophets long ago. We are made right with God by placing our faith in Jesus Christ. And this is true for everyone who believes, no matter who we are. For everyone has sinned; we all fall short of God's glorious standard. **Yet God freely and graciously declares that we are righteous. He did this through Christ Jesus when he freed us from the penalty for our sins. For God presented Jesus as the sacrifice for sin.** *People are made right with God when they believe that Jesus sacrificed his life, shedding his blood. This sacrifice shows that God was being fair when he held back and did not punish those who sinned in times past, for he was looking ahead and including them in what he would do in this present time. God did this to demonstrate his righteousness, for he himself is fair and just,* *and he declares sinners to be right in his sight when they believe in Jesus.* (Romans 3:21-26 NLT)

Unearned Forgiveness

For he hath made him to be sin for us, who knew no sin; that we might be made the righteousness of God in him. (2 Corinthians 5:21)

S in interrupted our relationship with God, but Jesus intervened and reconciled us back to the Father. Adam fell and Jesus took the fall so that we could stand in right standing before God. We are accepted in the beloved because the beloved, Jesus, was an acceptable sacrifice to God. The blood of Jesus is totally acceptable as complete satisfaction for the sinful violation of God's righteousness caused by the disobedience of our first family.

Jesus justified the believer at Calvary through the shedding of His blood. To justify is to be declared righteous before God. Justification is God declaring righteous those who trust Jesus as their Lord and Savior. This righteousness is based on the righteousness of Christ being imputed to the accounts of those who confess their sins, believe Jesus is the Son of God, and invite Him in to their hearts.

ALL ROADS LEAD TO CALVARY AND THE CROSS LEADS TO FORGIVENESS.

According as he hath chosen us in him before the foundation of the world, that we should be holy and without blame before him in love: Having predestinated us unto the

> *adoption of children by Jesus Christ to himself,* ***according to the good pleasure of his will, to the praise of the glory of his grace, wherein he hath made us accepted in the beloved. In whom we have redemption through the blood, the forgiveness of sins, according to the riches in his grace.*** (Ephesians 1:4-7 emphasis added)

Most people have the idea that God will forgive us of our sins simply because we ask Him. What they may not understand is that the basis for our forgiveness is not our request, but Christ's payment of our debt. God cannot forgive wrongs just because someone asks. His holiness will not allow Him to overlook sin; it must be punished. His justice will not allow Him to forgive sin without a payment. Sin has wages that must be paid. Everyone has sinned; we all fall short of God's glorious standard.

Only with the substitutionary death of the perfect lamb, the Son of God, does the Father have a legitimate basis by which He can forgive whoever comes to Him in faith and repentance. There is nothing we can do to earn His forgiveness. Forgiveness is granted only when Christ's blood is applied to our lives. We cannot pay our sin-debt, Jesus paid it for us. Without His intervention, we have no hope of forgiveness and salvation.

> *You were dead because of your sins and because your sinful nature was not yet cut away. Then God made you alive with Christ, for he forgave all our sins.* ***He canceled the record of the charges against us and took it away by nailing it to the cross.*** (Colossians 2:13-14 NLT emphasis added)

At the cross our deliverance from the penalty of death and eternal separation from God was purchased. The works of men do not bring about salvation. Grace and works are distinct and completely opposite. For this reason, salvation can never be the mixture of the two.

> *And since it is through God's kindness, then it is not by their good works. For in that case, God's grace would not be what it really is—free and undeserved.* (Romans 11:6 NLT)

The Forgiveness of God

> *Because of the joy awaiting him,* **he endured the cross, disregarding its shame.** *Now he is seated in the place of honor beside God's throne.* (Hebrews 12:2 NLT emphasis added)

Jesus' death on the cross was sacrificial, substitutionary, and sufficient. He did it all in obedience to the Father. He knew why He came and what He was to do. He made the choice to suffer the pain and humiliation of the cross to pay for the forgiveness of our sins knowing the joy awaiting Him.

Sacrificial: Jesus gave His life and laid it down. He gave it up as an offering for our sins. In John 10:18; Jesus said, "No one can take my life from me, **I sacrifice it voluntarily.** For I have the authority to lay it down when I want to and also to take it up again. For this is what my Father has commanded" (NLT emphasis added).

Substitutionary: He took our place. "He personally carried our sins in his body on the cross so that we can be dead to sin and live for what is right. By his wounds you and I are healed" (1 Peter 2:24 NLT).

Sufficient: He made total provision for the forgiveness of our sin. "**Christ suffered for our sins once for all time.** He never sinned, but he died for sinners to bring you safely home to God. He suffered physical death, but he was raised to life in the Spirit" (1 Peter 3:18 NLT emphasis added).

> *Even as David also describeth the blessedness of the man, unto whom God imputeth righteousness without works, Saying, Blessed are they whose iniquities are forgiven, and whose sins are covered. Blessed is the man to whom the Lord will not impute sin.* (Romans 4:6-8)

We received God's forgiveness the moment we are enabled of the Holy Spirit to trust Christ as our Savior from sin, confessed our need for forgiveness, and asked Jesus to be our Lord and Savior. Our forgiveness is complete because of our justification in Christ by which God declared us righteous in His Son. Imputed means to pass to one's account. In this case, Jesus placed His righteousness upon our record and into our account when we trusted upon Him for salvation.

> *As far as the east is from the west, so far hath he removed our transgressions from us.* (Psalm 103:12)

Two Types of Forgiveness

There are two types of forgiveness spoken of in scripture: Judicial and Fatherly. Judicial is from the courtroom and fatherly is from the home. Judicial forgiveness deals with our conversion (position) while fatherly forgiveness deals with our sanctification (practice). Judicial forgiveness takes place once and for all at the time of conversion. Then we need to experience God's fatherly forgiveness for the sins we continue to commit as born again believers.

> *Who dares accuse us whom God has chosen for his own? No one—for God himself has given us right standing with himself. Who then will condemn us? No one—for Christ Jesus died for us and was raised to life for us, and he is sitting in the place of honor at God's right hand, pleading for us.* (Romans 8:33-34 NLT)

First let us go to the courtroom. God is the Judge and sinful man is the person on trial. Man is guilty of sinning and the penalty is eternal death. But the Lord Jesus appears and announces, "I will pay the penalty which man's sins deserve and I will die as a substitute for him!" This is what the Savior did on the Cross of Calvary. Now the Judge announces to sinful man, "If you will surrender to my Son as your Lord and Savior, I will forgive you." As soon as the man puts his faith in the Savior, he receives judicial forgiveness of all his sins. He will never have to pay the punishment for them in hell because Christ has paid it all. The forgiven sinner now enters into a new relationship. God is no longer his Judge, now He is his Father.

> *And you, being dead in your sins and the uncircumcision of your flesh, hath he quickened together with him, having forgiven you all trespasses.* (Colossians 2:13)

Though we have been completely forgiven the punishment of our sin by God the righteous judge through salvation in Christ, we need to regularly experience God's fatherly forgiveness for the sins we continue to commit as born again believers. Judicial forgiveness deals with our conversion (position) while fatherly forgiveness deals with our sanctification (practice).

Fatherly forgiveness takes place every time a believer confesses and repents of his or her sin. This is what Jesus taught in John 13:8-10.

> *"No," Peter protested, "you will never ever wash my feet!" Jesus replied, "Unless I wash you, you won't belong to me." Simon Peter exclaimed, "Then wash my hands and head as well, Lord, not just my feet!" Jesus replied, "A person who has bathed all over does not need to wash, except for the feet, to be entirely clean. And you disciples are clean, but not all of you."* (NLT)

We need the bath of regeneration only once to deliver us from the penalty of sins, but we need many cleansings throughout our Christian lives to give us fatherly forgiveness. All past, present, and future sins are forgiven by grace through faith in Jesus Christ in justification. This is what it means to be saved (past tense), and this is also the beginning of sanctification. We can't and don't have one without the other.

> *For I say, through grace given unto me, to every man that is among you, not to think of himself more highly than he ought to think; but to think soberly, according as God hath dealt to every man the measure of faith.* (Romans 12:3)

So now we move into the home for an illustration of fatherly forgiveness. God is the Father and the believer is the child. In an unguarded moment of weakness, the child commits an act of sin. Then what happens? Does God sentence the child to die for the sin? Of course not because God is no longer the judge, but the Father. What does happen then? The child has not lost his salvation, but he has lost the joy of his salvation. He may experience the discipline of his loving Father, which is designed to bring him back into joyous fellowship. As soon as the child confesses his sin, he receives fatherly forgiveness.

We must daily confess our sins. The word "confess" is *homologeo*, which means to agree with. We must align and agree with God's word. Our confession impacts our intimacy with God. It deals with our daily experiential walk. A believer's confession of sin is not for the Father's benefit but for ours.

While justification secures our salvation in the past, sanctification secures it in the present as the Holy Spirit completes the work He began in us at our time of conversion. Sanctification is the ongoing work of the Holy Spirit, to work in and through us to do God's will, the good works that were prepared in advance for us to accomplish. The Holy Spirit convicts us of sin, leads us to repentance, and cleanses us from all unrighteousness.

Glorification is the Christian's future, in which we will be saved from the presence of sin, and righteousness will be impeccable, we will be one with God, even as Jesus prayed to the Father (John 17). Finally, in heaven, our "state" of righteousness will be saints, even as we now stand as righteous through justification by grace through faith in Jesus Christ.

Putting It to Rest

"Up in the church tower," he said, nodding out the window, "is a bell which is rung by pulling on a rope. But after one lets go of the rope the bell keeps on swinging. First, ding, then, dong, slower and slower until there's a final dong, and it stops. I believe the same thing is true of forgiveness. When we forgive, we take our hand off the rope. But if we've been tugging at our grievances for a long time, we mustn't be surprised if the old angry thoughts keep coming for a while. They're just the ding-dongs of the old bell slowing down." – Corrie ten Boom

We are to be mirrors of God's forgiving grace to us, reflecting to others the forgiveness we ourselves have already received. Sometimes this process takes some time to accomplish in our lives. We know what we want to do, but we also are aware we need the guidance of the Holy Spirit to truly accomplish God's purpose in our lives.

> *Forbearing one another, and forgiving one another, if any man have a quarrel against any: even as Christ forgave you, so also do ye.* (Colossians 3:13)

Everything Changed at the Cross

Before the cross we forgave to be forgiven, but after the cross, the Bible teaches that we are to forgive because we have been forgiven. The level to which we forgive others rather than demand that our wrath be satisfied is the clearest indication of how fully our hearts have been gripped by the gospel and the forgiveness God has extended to us. We demonstrate how fully we grasp our forgiveness in Christ by how fully we love and forgive others.

It is proper to say that God has completely forgiven all our sin – past, present, and even the future. As a result, born again believers are not under wrath and judgment, condemned to die, nor from the point of our salvation destined for hell. Paul says, "There is therefore now no condemnation for those who are in Christ Jesus" (Roman 8:1).

The Righteous Judge has declared us pardoned, justified, and righteous. No human including ourselves or any demonic principality can condemn us or lay any charge against us. Our job is to go and extend this same level of forgiveness to others, not because they deserve it but because of God's forgiveness of us when we did not deserve it.

> *My little children, these things write I unto you, that ye sin not. And if any man sin, we have an advocate with the Father, Jesus Christ the righteous: And he is the propitiation for our sins: and not for ours only, but also for the sins of the whole world. Brethren, I write no new commandment unto you, but an old commandment which ye had from the beginning. The old commandment is the word which ye have heard from the beginning.* (1 John 2:1-2, 7)

Defining Moments

> *For everyone has sinned; we all fall short of God's glorious standard.* ***Yet God freely and graciously declares that we are righteous. He did this through Christ Jesus when he freed us from the penalty for our sins. For God presented Jesus as the sacrifice for sin.*** (Romans 3:23-25 NLT emphasis added)

Everything Changed at the Cross

Before the cross you forgave to be forgiven, but after the cross, the Bible teaches that you are to forgive because you have been forgiven. The level to which you forgive others rather than demand that your wrath be satisfied is the clearest indication of how fully your heart has been gripped by the gospel and the forgiveness God has extended to you even though you did not deserve it. You demonstrate how fully you grasp your forgiveness in Christ by how fully you love and forgive others.

> *Heal the sick, raise the dead, cure those with leprosy, and cast out demons.* **Give as freely as you have received!** (Matthew 10:8 NLT emphasis added)

It's Time to Ask Yourself:

> *Am I a mirror of God's forgiving grace to me?*
> *Do I reflect to others the forgiveness I have already received?*
> *Do I freely give as I have received?*
> *How fully do I love and forgive others?*
> *For if ye forgive men their trespasses, your heavenly Father will also forgive you: but if ye forgive not men their trespasses, neither will your Father forgive your trespasses.* (Matthew 6:14-15)

Conclusion

Underneath Unforgiveness

When angry, do not sin; do not let your wrath (your exasperation, your fury or indignation) last until the sun goes down. Leave no such room or foothold for the devil give no opportunity to him. (Ephesians 4:26-27 AMP)

Anger is a strong feeling of intense displeasure, hostility, or indignation that results from a real or imagined threat, insult, frustration, or injustice toward yourself or others important to you. So often behind anger lies fear. An angry person can appear to be strong and in control. However, fear can reside underneath anger. Anger and fear are considered in many ways to be the same mind state, just in different forms. Anger is the outflowing expression while fear is held within.

Anger can devastate marriages, separate children and parents, and poison other relationships. There are three categories of anger: rage, resentment, and indignation.

Rage is uncontrolled or explosive anger and is usually the result of a longstanding issue. Rage can also be viewed as open warfare against another. It can also be known as "Powder Keg Anger." Anyone in its path, such as a spouse or child, is usually taken by surprise.

Resentment is suppressed or repressed anger. We might think of resentment as guerrilla warfare. It is passive aggression and possibly worse than rage. "Crockpot Anger" simmers and boils for a long time. Some people may be in complete denial about their stewing emotion or may take pride in possessing the ability to control their behavior. But denied anger is like a poison – spiritually, emotionally, and physically.

> "Forgiveness is more powerful than anger. Anger is a reaction to feelings of impotence. It is an attempt to grasp the power we feel we have lost. Forgiveness, though it may appear weak, is actually strong. It takes a powerful position of change, defines the self anew, and refuses to be dominated and overwhelmed by another's evil acts." – David Augsburger[8]

Indignation is generally directed toward conditions or circumstances, not directly at another person. However, it can lead to trying to do something to right a wrong.

Anger can be caused by not getting our way or when we lose control of a situation. Feeling rejected, being excluded, overlooked, or mistreated can also stir up hostility. Losing what we cherish or simply fearing that loss can make us angry. Disappointment and unmet expectations can lead to frustration and then anger. When we see people mistreated, we can become indignant on their behalf. Comparing our life to the lives of others may give us feelings of inadequacy which can breed the seeds of anger.

---

[8] David Augsburger entitled; "The New Freedom of Forgiveness" 2000; Moody Press.

Whatever the cause, anger gives the enemy a foothold and provides a base for further negative advancement. We give place to the devil when we fail to confront our fear, do not deal correctly with our anger, and refuse to resolve our unforgiveness issues.

If our rights are constantly violated and if we don't manage to channel the resulting anger correctly, we can end up depressed. Suppressed emotions can be one of the main reasons causing depression. People who manage to properly channel their suppressed emotions in a timely manner are less likely to get depressed. If any of this manifests in our lives, we need to look underneath the outward behavior to find the true cause of that behavior.

What Is Underneath Your Story?

Our story usually flows from a motif or theme that has traveled through most of our encounters on our life's journey. Joseph experienced his life motif within the crux of "injustice" and "forgiveness." He seemed to be encapsulated in God's preordained destiny for his life. Jabez, Job, and Jonah all dealt with pain and suffering in their lives and how they handled it deeply affected whether they fulfilled their true God-given destiny in life.

We are created within a God ordained family. All parts are interrelated and each part impacts another part. Much of what we respond to or react to can be traced to our family of origin story. It is vitally important that we each take the time to reflect on and consider our family of origin. We will learn why we react and respond to certain events and even why we find it hard to extend forgiveness for specific types of hurts or offenses perpetrated against us through a study of our family tree. Generational curses are very real and need to be dealt with so they are not allowed to continue to grow and affect future generations.

One thing we must remember is that all pain is redemptive when placed in the hand of God. The cure for pain is found in the pain. We cannot escape the dilemmas of this life, but however great our struggle, God is greater. God's hand of grace and mercy are always at work.

Forgiveness is an issue of the heart and is supernatural in its movement. It is a choice you and I must make each and every day. How we choose can make the difference whether we remain **Imprisoned Within** and *Stuck in Unforgiveness* or move forward into our God-given purpose and abundant life.

Defining Moment

The challenge for you today is "Do you really want to be made whole and well?" (John 5:6)

Begin by making Psalm 51:10 your prayer.

Then study these verses and record what the Holy Spirit reveals to you from each one about your heart issues and how you are dealing with unforgiveness issues deep down inside of you.

Matthew 12:34 says from the outflow of the _____ the _____ _____.
What message are you sending out to those around you?

1 Corinthians 14:25 warns us that the _____ of the heart will be _____ _____.
What might this reveal about you especially in the area of unforgiveness?

Psalm 51:17 says God is looking for what kind of heart? _____
Does this describe your heart?

Why is the condition of your heart so important? (see Proverbs 27:19)
_____

Will you pray and ask God to give you an undivided heart that you may walk in His truth and move forward to fulfill your God-given destiny? (Psalm 86:11)

> *Dear heavenly Father, I come to You in the precious name of Jesus. I recognize that You are a God of great grace and can do the seemingly impossible. Lord, I pray that You will search my heart and enlighten me with Your Holy Spirit. Allow Your Spirit to bring any area of darkness and unforgiveness to the surface of my knowing and deliver me. I pray for a uniting of head and heart around Your precepts and Your holy Word. My desire is to please You and to complete the assignment You have placed on my life. I trust You God to do great things in my life for the advancement of Your Kingdom. Amen*

About the Author

Apostle Kimberly Nixon currently resides in Cameron, North Carolina with Michael, her husband of thirty-five years. She has a wonderful son, two beautiful daughters, and two blessed grandchildren. Apostle Nixon currently leads Williams Chapel Church in Spring Lake, North Carolina. Its mission is to create a safe place for a shared vision of healing, hope, and reconciliation. Her focus of ministry and the passion of her heart is within the call to International missions. Apostle Nixon may be contacted at worship@wclive.org or by visiting Williams Chapel's webpage at www.wclive.org.

www.ingramcontent.com/pod-product-compliance
Ingram Content Group UK Ltd.
Pitfield, Milton Keynes, MK11 3LW, UK
UKHW041954230426
12048UKWH00008B/340